NORWEGIAN, SWEDISH, AND DANISH IMMIGRANTS

1820-1920

by Kay Melchisedech Olson

Content Consultant:
Dr. Roland Thorstensson, Professor of Scandinavian Studies
Gustavus Adolphus College
St. Peter, Minnesota

Blue Earth Books

an imprint of Capstone Press
Mankato, Minnesota

Blue Earth Books are published by Capstone Press
151 Good Counsel Drive, P.O. Box 669, Mankato, Minnesota 56002
http://www.capstone-press.com

Library of Congress Cataloging-in-Publication Data

Olson, Kay Melchisedech.
  Norwegian, Swedish, and Danish Immigrants, 1820–1920 / by Kay Melchisedech Olson
      p. cm. – (Coming to America)
  Includes bibliographical references (p. 31) and index.
  ISBN 0-7368-0798-5
  1. Norwegian Americans—History—Juvenile literature. 2. Swedish Americans—History—Juvenile literature. 3. Danish Americans—History—Juvenile literature. 4. Immigrants—United States—History—Juvenile literature. 5. United States—Emigration and immigration—History—Juvenile literature. 6. Norway—Emigration and immigration—History—Juvenile literature. 7. Sweden—Emigration and immigration—History—Juvenile literature. 8. Denmark—Emigration and immigration—History—Juvenile literature. [1. Norwegian Americans—History. 2. Swedish Americans—History. 3. Danish Americans—History. 4. United States—Emigration and immigration—History. 5. Norway—Emigration and immigration—History. 6. Sweden—Emigration and immigration—History. 7. Denmark—Emigration and immigration—History.] I. Title II. Series.
  E184.S2 O45 2002
  305.9'0691'0973—dc21   00-013245

Summary: Discusses reasons Scandinavian people left their homeland to come to America, the experiences immigrants had in the new country, and the contributions this cultural group made to American society. Includes sidebars and activities.

Editorial credits
Designer: Heather Kindseth
Photo Researcher: Heidi Schoof
Product Planning Editor: Lois Wallentine

Photo credits
Minnesota Historical Society, cover, 4, 7 (left), 11, 13, 16, 18, 21, 22, 25, 26 (right), 29 (both); The Danish Museum, an International Cultural Center, 7 (right), 14 (left); Brian Vikander/CORBIS, 9; Gregg Andersen, flag images, 10, 23, 26 (left); The American Swedish Institute, 14 (right); Library of Congress, 15; Fred Hultstrand History in Pictures Collection, NDIRS-NDSU, Fargo, 20

2 3 4 5 6 07 06 05 04 03 02

Contents

Chapter 1—Early Scandinavian Immigrants 4

Chapter 2—Life in the Old Country 8

Chapter 3—The Trip Over 12

Chapter 4—Arriving in America 16

Chapter 5—Surviving in America 20

Chapter 6—Keeping Traditions 24

Features

Immigration Route Map 5

Route to the Midwest Map 17

Make a Family Tree 27

Timeline 28

Famous Scandinavian Americans 29

Words to Know 30

To Learn More 31

Places to Write and Visit 31

Internet Sites 32

Index 32

NORWEGIAN SWEDISH & DANISH IMMIGRANTS 1820 TO 1920

EARLY SCANDINAVIAN IMMIGRANTS

Before 1800, only a few Scandinavians emigrated from their homes in Norway, Sweden, and Denmark to live in other countries. In 1637, a group of Swedish immigrants settled the area that later became the state of Delaware. They called their colony New Sweden. But during the 1700s and early 1800s, laws restricting emigration made leaving their country difficult for Swedish citizens. Until 1850, only about 20,000 Norwegians had come to the United States.

Cleng Peerson was one of the first Scandinavian immigrants to come to America. Peerson, who was born in Norway in 1783, was one of two Quakers who went to America in 1821. Their goal was to find a place for a Quaker church congregation to settle in the United States. Peerson's companion, Knud Olsen Eide, died after arriving in America. But in 1824, Peerson went back to Norway and told church members about the good opportunities that America had to offer.

In 1925, Norwegian Americans from Minnesota posed in front of a sloop. In the mid-1800s, many Norwegian immigrants crossed the Atlantic Ocean in sloops similar to this one.

Immigration Route

Atlantic Ocean

SWEDEN

NORWAY

SCOTLAND

• Gothenburg

DENMARK

ENGLAND

GERMANY

• New York City

UNITED
STATES

From 1820 to 1920, about 2.5 million Scandinavians left their homes in Norway, Sweden, and Denmark. Norwegians and Swedes often left from Gothenburg while Danes left from ports in Germany. Early immigrants sailed first to England, Scotland, or Germany. They then transferred to ships bound for America. Later immigrants usually sailed directly from their home country to the United States.

Peerson brought the first group of immigrants to America on a sloop called the *Restauration.* Their trip across the Atlantic Ocean took 98 days. This group of about 50 people became known as Sloopers. Some of the Sloopers were Quakers, and others sympathized with the Quaker religion. The Sloopers who left Norway for America in 1825 were in search of religious freedom.

These new Scandinavian immigrants wrote letters to people back home. They told friends and family members about the laws that separated church and state in America. They described the rich farming land in the Midwest. People in Norway copied and recopied these letters, sharing them with villagers around the Norwegian countryside. The letters that Peerson's Sloopers sent home convinced many more people to emigrate from Norway to America. Cleng Peerson became known as the father of Norwegian immigration.

Ole Rynning also convinced many Norwegians to leave Norway for America. In 1837, Rynning settled in Illinois, about 75 miles (120 kilometers) south of Chicago. During his first winter in America, Rynning suffered frostbite in the region's cold temperatures. He wrote a book during his recovery and called it *A True Account of America for the Information and Help of Peasant and Commoner*. In 1839, Rynning's book was published in Norway, and many people who read it decided to go to America.

When the Swedish government changed its law limiting emigration, many middle-class Swedes left for America. Students, merchants, government workers, and intellectuals were the first to leave their Swedish homeland. Like the Norwegians before them, the Swedish immigrants sent letters from the United States to friends and family. Swedish newspapers printed many of these letters. They described America as a paradise on Earth. These glowing accounts of cheap land and plenty of jobs convinced many more Swedes to leave for America.

From 1851 to 1930, about 1.2 million people left Sweden for America. In the late 1800s, so many young people and their families emigrated that Sweden's birthrate was slower than its death rate. Emigration from Sweden almost completely emptied some Swedish towns and villages.

In the 100 years from 1820 to 1920, almost 3.5 million Scandinavians left their homeland to come to the United States. In 1820, Norway's total population was about 1 million people. By 1925, almost 800,000 Norwegians had left their country to settle in America. In the years from 1868 to 1873, at least 100,000 Swedes left to start a new life in the United States. By the end of the 1920s, about 1.2 million Swedish people and more than 250,000 Danes had come to America.

Swedes in America built sturdy cabins (left) by notching and stacking logs to form solid walls. Danes brought a skill for making warm shoes from reeds (below). They made the shoes by braiding hollow reeds into strips and sewing the strips together.

By 1990, about 11.5 million people of Scandinavian descent were part of the United States' population. That number is about half of the current population of Norway, Sweden, and Denmark combined.

Their habits of hard work and thrift helped make Scandinavian immigrants successful in the United States.

Many new immigrants had been farmers or field laborers in their homeland, and they knew how to work the land and grow crops. They worked hard and saved as much money as they could. Although they sailed across the ocean with few possessions, most Scandinavian immigrants made a good life for themselves in America.

LIFE IN THE OLD COUNTRY

The snowflake pattern is a common design in Norwegian knitting.

In the 1800s, most people living in Norway, Sweden, and Denmark were farmers. They grew crops such as barley, oats, and rye. They raised cattle, sheep, chickens, pigs, and other livestock.

Life was not easy for these Scandinavian farmers. The climate in northern European countries was challenging. Winters were long and cold, while the summer growing season was short. Many farmers rented small plots, which usually were no more than 2 acres (.8 hectare) of land. They had to give the landowner a portion of their harvest as payment for using the farmland.

Most Scandinavians had large families who lived in small cottages. The children helped with farm chores by working in the fields or tending herds of cattle and sheep. Children sometimes found jobs outside the home. They earned extra money by spinning and weaving wool or setting and tending fish traps.

In the northernmost parts of Scandinavia, winters last six months or more. During this half of the year, the sun offers only about seven hours of light each day to Earth's northern regions. Families earned a living during the long winters by making items to sell. Fathers and sons often built cabinets and carved items out of wood. Mothers and daughters knit stockings, caps, and sweaters. But few people could afford to pay money for these goods at the local market. Many times families had to bring their handmade items home with no money to show for their work.

Some Scandinavian immigrants left behind the Norwegian fjords and mountains, such as Sognefjorden in Balestrand, Norway (below). Others left the lakes and forests of Sweden, and the low flat, grasslands of Denmark. They settled in areas of America that reminded them of their homeland.

"All those who have been in America for a few years, with a few individual exceptions are in a contented and independent position. Anxiety and care with respect to daily bread and subsistence for their families burden them no longer . . . They do not suffer want . . . The majority still live in their original log cabins, which, however, are always a good deal better than the mountain huts in which they lived in Norway . . . They have only a little money . . . the crops are not yet sufficient to supply the needs of all the settlers . . ."

—J. R. Reiersen, 1844 (from his Norwegian handbook about America)

Scandinavian families worked hard but they also had time for fun. Because summers were so short, Scandinavians made the most of the season with a celebration called Midsummerfest. Families cut sapling trees to decorate the outside of their houses. They made little outdoor rooms of saplings and branches called leaf houses. In the summer, mothers sometimes served meals in the leaf houses, and children often slept there.

Christmas was another happy time for Scandinavian families. This holiday season often lasted 20 days. Neighbors held parties and invited each other to celebrate. Every family cut down a pine tree and brought it into the house to decorate with handmade ornaments. They cut out paper stars and made paper chains to hang on the tree. To light the tree, they fastened candles to the branches. People also wove tiny baskets out of paper strips and filled them with candy, raisins, or nuts to hang on the tree. They waited until after Christmas to eat these treats as they took down the tree.

In the mid-1800s, Scandinavian families who rented farmland often struggled to pay taxes to the landowner. They also paid their church minister a head tax for every adult living in the community. Families often were heavily in debt. They sometimes paid their taxes with goods such as grain and livestock or butter and cheese. But when the crops failed or their animals became sick and died, the Scandinavian people had little to eat and few goods to pay their taxes.

People wove paper strips into tiny baskets and filled them with nuts. They hung these decorations from Christmas tree branches.

10

Royalty ruled Scandinavian countries. The kings often had absolute power. Each country had a national religion, and all other forms of worship were outlawed. Men had to serve in the military, whether or not their families needed them to work on the farm. Only people of noble or high birth were allowed to own land. The Scandinavian governments did not allow peasant farmers to own land.

In the late 1860s, Sweden suffered three years of trouble. Sweden's climate generally is sunnier and drier than other Scandinavian countries. But in 1867, too much rain fell in Sweden, causing much of the grain crop to rot. This wet year was followed by a very dry year. In 1868, so little rain fell in Sweden that many of the farm crops burned under the hot sun. After two years of failed crops, many Swedes were weak from starvation. The "severe year" followed in 1869. A number of disease epidemics spread through the population, killing thousands of people. About 40,000 people left Sweden for America that year.

Conditions continued to worsen in Scandinavia. The population in the region was growing faster than the food supply. Families grew poorer and many people were starving. At the same time, the United States offered people religious freedom, rich farmland at cheap prices, and a democratic form of government. Many poor and hungry Scandinavians were willing to leave their homes for the chance of a better life in America.

Posters advertised transportation between America and Scandinavian countries. Many people started their journey with a train trip to a port city where they boarded passenger ships.

THE TRIP OVER

"The passengers had boarded the Franklin *on the evening of 8 April. Below deck they found 160 bunks which were wide enough for three persons to lie side by side . . . On Sunday the cooks served sweet soup; Monday, pea soup; Tuesday and Wednesday, rice; Friday, barley mush; and Saturday, herring and potatoes."*

—Anthon H. Lund, a
Danish immigrant
on board the Franklin, 1862

Until the 1900s, there were almost no boats to carry passengers directly from Scandinavian countries to New York or other U.S. ports. Many southern Norwegian and Swedish emigrants took a train to Gothenburg, Sweden. From there they sailed to England, Scotland, or Germany and boarded a boat to America. Danish emigrants usually sailed from a German port.

In the early 1800s, there were no laws governing conditions on sailing ships. The trip from Europe to America took several months. Passengers could never be sure how the food or living quarters would be. English and German ship owners decided what supplies to take on the voyage. Scandinavian immigrants were not always familiar with the foods that were served on board. Some of the food contained bugs and spoiled during the voyage. Some immigrants said they had to eat food that pigs would refuse.

The least costly tickets on the immigrant ships were in the steerage section, an area located one or more floors below the main deck. Here conditions were crowded, noisy, dark, and smelly. Three or more people shared hard, uncomfortable beds stacked one on top of another. There was no room to wash or bathe. Many of the men on board smoked or chewed tobacco, and the air often was smoky and stuffy.

Passengers often became sick on the voyage. Most immigrants had never sailed on the ocean and suffered from seasickness. Other people became sick from eating spoiled food or drinking germ-filled water. Some passengers were already sick when they boarded, and their diseases spread to others on the ship.

Immigrants from many different countries sometimes sailed on the same boat. Passengers spoke different languages and often did not understand one another. Immigrants of one country sometimes stole the money and valuables from the immigrants of another country.

There also were happy times on the voyage to America. Young couples decided to marry. They had the ship's captain perform the ceremony on board. Women gave birth to babies during the voyage. Mothers and fathers told children stories and played games to help pass the time. Many immigrants took out the letters they had received from relatives in America and read them over and over again.

New York was the most popular port of entry into the United States for Scandinavian immigrants. They passed through customs, declaring the few

When the weather was fair, immigrants could go up on deck to get some fresh air.

13

"The food on the boat consisted of soup, potatoes, beans, fish, bread, or hardtack biscuits. The cooking was done in iron pots so large the cook could get inside. No bread was made on the ship, the biscuits having been made months before and were extremely hard and dry. The potatoes were sour and soggy. The drinking water was taken from the River Elbe, in Germany, put in wooden barrels, and was as black as coal when we drank it."

—Olaf Jensen, a Scandinavian steerage passenger aboard the Humboldt, *1866*

⭐

Scandinavian immigrants packed useful items and keepsakes in their travel trunks. People often brought cooking pots, candle holders, cloth, mittens, socks, and shoes. The brass iron from Denmark is engraved with the initials "K.K.L.D." and the year "1852."

possessions they had brought across the ocean. Each family usually had a trunk filled with a Bible, some clothes, cooking utensils, tools, and a few keepsakes, such as embroidered linen or photographs. Immigrants also had to show their passports or travel documents and pass a quick health examination. They then were on their own to begin a new life in America.

★ Castle Garden ★

On August 1, 1855, the State of New York opened Castle Garden as the first landing station for immigrants. It was located on the southwestern tip of Manhattan in New York City, and had been the site of a military fort. Later it was used as a concert hall.

After leaving the boat, passengers waited in line to pass through customs at Castle Garden. The immigrants sometimes rested on benches, heated tea or coffee on nearby radiators, or looked for jobs advertised in newspapers. Sick immigrants received medical attention. Healthy immigrants could exchange their foreign money and find information about housing and transportation in the United States.

By the late 1800s, about 566,000 Scandinavians and hundreds of thousands of other immigrants had passed through Castle Garden. It was not big enough to handle the growing number of immigrants to America. The federal government took over immigration processing and moved it to Ellis Island in 1892. Ellis Island is in Upper New York Bay, where many immigrants first looked at America.

ARRIVING IN AMERICA

In 1840, a Norwegian magazine published an article about a group of Scandinavian immigrants who arrived in Boston, Massachusetts. The article said people in Boston were surprised to see immigrants getting off the boat looking so much "like other human beings." Bostonians expected the Scandinavians to be dressed in animal furs. Immigrants sometimes did arrive in America wearing colorful costumes of their homeland. But most of them dressed like typical American farmers.

The immigrants faced another long journey after they left the boat and passed through customs. Between 1850 and 1890, most of the Scandinavian immigrants headed to the Upper Midwest, an area that includes the present-day states of Minnesota, Iowa, Illinois, Wisconsin, North Dakota, and South Dakota. The region's climate, rich farmland, and many lakes had already attracted settlements of Scandinavians. Newly arrived immigrants often went first to live with family and friends who already were settled.

Immigrants arriving in New York generally bought tickets to ride by boat up the Hudson River. The boat traveled through the Erie Canal and on to the Great Lakes. Many of these Scandinavian immigrants settled in or near Chicago.

Early Scandinavian immigrants usually wore work clothes typical of American farmers. But on special occasions, they dressed in clothes styled from their homes in Norway, Sweden, and Denmark.

North Dakota

Minnesota

South Dakota

Lake Superior

Wisconsin

Lake Huron

Iowa

Lake Michigan

Lake Ontario

New York

Erie Canal

Hudson River

Lake Erie

Chicago

Illinois

New York City

Route to the Midwest

Immigrants rode barges up the Hudson River, west along the Erie Canal, and through the Great Lakes to reach the Upper Midwest.

In 1884, about 10,000 people in Chicago were Swedish. So many Swedish immigrants settled in Chicago that an area of the city became known as Swede Town.

In 1852, the great number of new Swedish immigrants coming to Chicago caused overcrowding. Large families rented small rooms in tenement buildings and boarding houses. The living conditions in these places often were dirty and full of disease. That summer, an epidemic of cholera broke out, making people sick with vomiting, diarrhea, and dehydration. In one five-room boarding house where 28 immigrants lived, 15 people died in a single week.

Living conditions in America often were more difficult than new immigrants had imagined. Letters they had read

reported a life in America that was better than it actually was. Some immigrants found working conditions harder than they expected. Others were disappointed in the many unbelievers they encountered who did not attend church.

In 1862, the U.S. Congress passed the Homestead Act. This law allowed anyone to file for a free parcel of land. Each parcel was 160 acres (65 hectares). Homesteaders had to build a house, dig a well, plow at least 10 acres (4 hectares), and live on the land. Many Scandinavians took advantage of the Homestead Act and became landowners.

Scandinavians found that different areas of the Midwest reminded them of home. Many Danish immigrants found the rolling hills of Wisconsin a perfect place to raise dairy cattle. Many Swedish men found work in lumber mills that supplied the growing city of Chicago. Minnesota's many lakes were a familiar sight for the Norwegians and Swedes. By 1900, these groups outnumbered any other immigrant group in Minnesota, making it the most Scandinavian state in the Union.

The American West also attracted Scandinavian immigrants. Some Swedish and Danish immigrants belonged to the Mormon faith. They headed for Utah, where many other Mormons had settled. Single men from Sweden traveled to Oregon and Washington to work in the lumber camps. There were so many Swedish-born loggers in the Pacific Northwest that the crosscut saw became known as a Swedish fiddle.

Scandinavian immigrants seemed to blend easily into American life. They quickly became active in politics. Many immigrants held government positions and were political leaders throughout the Midwest.

By 1890, many Scandinavian Americans were busy farming the land of America's Midwest. The work was hard. But in their new homeland, immigrants could own their land and worship however they pleased.

Scandinavian Flags

Norway, Sweden, and Denmark all are located in northern Europe. Ancient Nordic people called this homeland Scandinavia. Each of the Scandinavian countries has its own flag. Scandinavian immigrants often brought small flags from their countries when they traveled to America.

Scandinavian flags share a similar design. Each flag has a sideways cross against a solid-color background. Some people believe this design is based on the banners once carried by Christian soldiers. You can draw and color a flag to represent each of the Scandinavian countries.

Denmark   Sweden   Norway

What You Need

plain white paper   pencil
ruler   crayons or colored pencils

What You Do

1. Lay a plain white sheet of paper the long way on a flat surface such as a desktop.
2. Use a ruler to guide you in making straight lines to form a sideways cross on the paper as shown.
3. Use crayons or colored pencils to color the flags. Follow the color designs shown for each Scandinavian country.

Flag Diagram for Norway

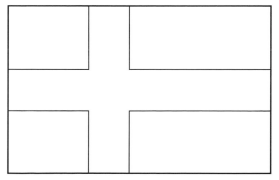

Flag Diagram for Denmark and Sweden

19

SURVIVING IN AMERICA

By the late 1800s, many Scandinavians were homesteading in America's Midwest. In 1896, Norwegian immigrant John Bakken and his family lived in this prairie sod house in North Dakota.

Scandinavian immigrants found that making a living in the United States sometimes was no easier than it had been back home. The Homestead Act offered free farmland to anyone who was willing to work for it. But immigrants and other pioneers often found that traveling to farming regions was a difficult job. Prairie land was mostly grass with a few rutty, dusty trails that served as roads. There were no bridges, and people had to cross rivers and streams.

When they reached their parcel of land, the immigrants had to build a house. Many Scandinavian immigrants were skilled carpenters, but they found few trees on the prairie. Instead of building log houses, many immigrants cut strips of prairie sod and stacked them like bricks. They called these sod houses "soddys."

The immigrants arrived at their homesteads with only the tools and supplies they could pack in wagons. They had to hurry to plow and plant their first crops before winter came. If their land was not near water, the immigrants had to dig wells by hand.

Immigrants found that farming in the United States was similar to farming back in their homeland. They were dependent on the weather. It sometimes rained too much and flooded the farmland. Other times drought shriveled the crops. But Scandinavian immigrants no longer had to pay taxes to a landowner as they had in their homeland. They also did not have to pay a head tax to a minister.

Scandinavian immigrants quickly adapted to life in America. They were part of almost every major event that shaped the country in the 1800s. Some Swedes and Norwegians joined the 49ers, traveling to California during the Gold Rush in the late 1840s and early 1850s. Some Scandinavians became soldiers. Most fought for the Union in the Civil War (1861–1865).

After the war, many Swedish-born Americans helped to build the country's first transcontinental railroad. First they worked on lines from the cities of St. Paul, Minnesota, and Chicago, Illinois. Later they helped lay railroad tracks farther to the west. After the east and west coasts were linked with an easy form of transportation, Scandinavian Americans settled throughout the United States.

Between 1890 and 1910, about 150,000 Swedes, Norwegians, and Danes settled along the Pacific coast. Many of these immigrants went into the lumber and

By 1880, many Scandinavian Americans had settled in the Midwest. This Norwegian immigrant family was comfortable in their new home in Ames, Iowa.

ship-building businesses in Washington and Oregon. Scandinavians who had lived close to the sea in their homeland worked in the salmon fisheries and canneries in California and Oregon. Others pioneered the fishing industry in Alaska.

By the late 1800s, many Scandinavian immigrants ran businesses in American cities. In 1890, Charles Samuelson operated this food store in Minneapolis.

Midwestern immigrant settlers continued to farm and raise livestock. When immigrants found it difficult to get good prices for their crops, they joined together. They formed farm cooperatives and agreed to sell their goods for the same fair price. When it was hard to afford the goods they needed, the Scandinavian immigrants formed retail cooperatives. They could buy goods at cheaper prices in bulk.

Danish farmers introduced new farming techniques to the egg and dairy industry in America. In 1882, a Danish immigrant in Iowa bought and used the first milk separator. This device separated the cream from cow's milk. In 1864, a Dane by the name of Christopher Nissen moved to Petaluma, California, and brought along an egg incubator. This invention hatched baby chicks more quickly than hens in the nest. Petaluma eventually became the center of California's poultry industry.

Some Scandinavian immigrants were craftspeople with skills in many different trades. Carpenters and stone masons worked in the building industries in cities such as New York, Chicago, San Francisco, Minneapolis, and Seattle. In 1871, almost all of Chicago was destroyed by a great fire. So many Swedish immigrants helped construct new buildings that many people said "the Swedes built Chicago." Scandinavian immigrants also worked in the mining industry. Many Norwegians mined copper and iron in Michigan and lead in Wisconsin.

Lindbergh's Favorite Swedish Party Cakes

★ ★

Charles Lindbergh, the son of a Swedish immigrant, was the first person to fly an airplane nonstop between New York and Paris, France. People often called Charles the "Lone Eagle" because he flew solo in his single-engine airplane. The Swedish butter cookie was one of young Charles' favorites. His mother called them "Swedish Party Cakes."

What You Need

Ingredients

1 pound (455 grams) butter

1 cup (250 mL) sugar

1 egg

2 teaspoons (10 mL) baking powder

1 teaspoon (5 mL) lemon or almond extract

4 cups (1 liter) flour

¼ cup (50 mL) sugar, for the dipping glass

Equipment

dry-ingredient measuring cups

mixing bowl

electric mixer

rubber spatula

measuring spoons

baking sheet

drinking glass

pot holders

metal spatula

wire cooling rack

What You Do

1. Remove butter from refrigerator and allow it to soften at room temperature.
2. Add butter, sugar, and 1 egg to mixing bowl. Mix well with electric mixer. Use a rubber spatula to scrape the inside of the bowl.
3. Add baking powder, lemon or almond extract, and 2 cups (500 mL) flour to ingredients in mixing bowl. Mix well.
4. Add remaining 2 cups (500 mL) flour and mix well.
5. Heat oven to 350°F (180°C).
6. With clean hands, roll cookie dough into 1-inch (2.5-centimeter) balls.
7. Place dough balls on baking sheet 2 inches (5 centimeters) apart.
8. Dip the bottom of the drinking glass in sugar. Flatten each ball with the bottom of the glass, dipping it in sugar as needed.
9. Bake 8 to 10 minutes. Remove baking sheet from oven with pot holders.
10. Using metal spatula, carefully remove the cookies from baking sheet and place on cooling rack.

Makes 30 to 36 cookies

23

KEEPING TRADITIONS

Rosemaling design

Scandinavians blended in well and made important contributions to American society. Many American traditions and customs have Nordic beginnings. A professional football team is called the Vikings. Special foods such as lutefisk and lefse are served on holidays. Nordic knitting, hardanger embroidery, and rosemaling painting have become popular crafts in America.

Religion was an important part of life in Scandinavia, and immigrants continued community worship in the United States. Many Swedes and Norwegians established Lutheran churches and schools. Some Danes and Swedes converted to the Mormon religion and settled in Utah after arriving in the United States.

Many Scandinavian immigrants were familiar with the democratic form of government and were eager to participate in U.S. politics. Scandinavian Americans served as representatives in the U.S. Congress, as governors, and on committees and boards devoted to improving agriculture. Two sons of Norwegian immigrants, Hubert Humphrey and Walter Mondale, served terms as vice president of the United States.

Scandinavians also have made important contributions to American business development. Conrad Hilton, son of a Norwegian immigrant, established the chain of hotels that now serve guests in almost all major cities of the world. Curtis Carlson, of Swedish descent, established the Radisson chain of hotels. Carl Erick Wickman was born in Sweden and immigrated to the United States when he was 17. He later founded the Greyhound Bus Lines in Hibbing, Minnesota.

By the 1920s, so many Scandinavians lived in Minnesota cities that it was called the most Scandinavian state in America. In 1925, shoppers in Minneapolis crowded outside Scandinavian window displays at a popular downtown department store.

By the 1900s, many Scandinavian Americans proudly marched in parades wearing the native dress and carrying flags of their native land.

Lefse is a favorite Scandinavian pastry.

Music always has been a part of Scandinavian life, especially performances by church choirs. Many Norwegian Americans have formed choral groups that perform at churches, festivals, and other entertainment events. The St. Olaf College choir in Northfield, Minnesota, is one of the most noted college choirs in America. Many Norwegian men's choirs still perform around the United States today.

Most Scandinavian American celebrations include the smörgasbord. This assortment of food combines modern recipes with traditional food. Lefse and lutefisk are favorite Scandinavian dishes. Lefse is a flat pastry made of potatoes, flour, butter, and whipping cream. Lutefisk is codfish preserved in lye and cooked and served with a whole boiled potato, sliced rutabagas, cream sauce, and melted butter.

★ Make a Family Tree ★

Genealogy is the study of family history. Genealogists often record this history in the form of a family tree. This chart records a person's ancestors, such as parents, grandparents, and great-grandparents.

Start your own family tree with the names of your parents and grandparents. Ask family members for their full names, including their middle names. Remember that your mother and grandmothers likely had a different last name before they were married. This name, called a maiden name, is probably the same as their fathers' last name.

Making a family tree helps you to know your ancestors and the countries from which they emigrated. Some people include the dates and places of birth with each name on their family tree. Knowing when and where these relatives were born will help you understand from which immigrant groups you have descended.

There are many ways to find information for your family tree. Ask for information from your parents, grandparents, and as many other older members of your family as you can. Some people research official birth and death records to find the full names of relatives. Genealogical societies often have information that will help with family tree research. If you know the cemetery where family members are buried, you may find some of the information you need on the gravestones.

Your father's mother

Your father's father

Your mother's father

Your mother's mother

Your father

Your mother

You

1800

1900

1825
Cleng Peerson brings a group of Norwegians called the Sloopers to live in America.

1848
Gold is discovered at Sutter's Mill. Some Scandinavian immigrants begin moving to California.

1884
About 10,000 Swedish immigrants are living in Chicago. Overcrowding in the city causes disease and epidemics.

1900
Scandinavians in Minnesota outnumber any other immigrant group in the state. Minnesota becomes known as the most Scandinavian state in the Union.

1925
A total of 800,000 Norwegians have immigrated to America.

1840
Swedish law changes, finally allowing citizens to emigrate.

1855
Castle Garden landing station opens in New York Harbor to help process new immigrants as they arrive in America.

1862
The Homestead Act is passed by the U.S. Congress, giving free land parcels to people willing to live and farm in the Midwest and on the western frontier.

1890
Minneapolis replaces Chicago as the main urban destination of Swedish immigrants.

1920
By the end of this decade, about 1.5 million Swedes are living in the United States.

1990
The U.S. census reports that 11.5 million people claim to be of Scandinavian descent.

★ **Charles A. Lindbergh** (1902–1974) The son of a Swedish immigrant father, Lindbergh was the first person to fly an airplane nonstop between New York and Paris. He made the trip by himself in 1927. The solo flight earned him the nickname the "Lone Eagle."

★ **Hubert H. Humphrey** (1911–1978) Born in Wallace, South Dakota, Humphrey was the grandson of Norwegian immigrants. Humphrey was active in politics and served as mayor of Minneapolis and senator from Minnesota. From 1965 to 1968, he served as vice president of the United States. Humphrey proposed medical care for the aged and helped win Senate approval of the nuclear test ban treaty and of the Civil Rights Act.

Charles A. Lindbergh

★ **Jacob Riis** (1849–1914) Born in Ribe, Denmark, Riis immigrated to the United States in 1870. Riis became America's first journalist-photographer. He took photographs that showed the terrible conditions in which many new immigrants lived in America.

★ **James Arness** (1923–) Born in Minneapolis to a Norwegian American family, Arness became well-known for his role of Marshal Matt Dillon on TV's *Gunsmoke*.

★ **Walter Mondale** (1928–) Born in Ceylon, Minnesota, Mondale is the son of a Norwegian American Methodist minister. He served as U.S. senator and supported open housing, busing for school integration, migrant worker protection, Indian education, and tax reform. In 1977, Mondale was inaugurated as vice president of the United States. As vice president, he supported legislation on labor-law reform.

Hubert H. Humphrey

29

Words to Know

ancestor (AN-sess-tur)—a member of one's family who lived a long time ago

aristocrat (uh-RISS-tuh-krat)—a member of a group of people thought to be the best in some way, usually based on how much money they have; aristocrats are members of the highest social rank or nobility.

customs (KUHSS-tuhms)—a checkpoint at a country's borders

emigrate (EM-uh-grate)—to leave your own country in order to live in another one

epidemic (ep-uh-DEM-ik)—an infectious disease that spreads quickly through a population

fjord (fee-ORD)—a long, narrow inlet of the ocean between high cliffs

genealogy (jee-nee-AL-uh-jee)—the study of family history

hardanger (HAR-dang-uhr)—fancy sewing that includes removing some threads from cloth and adding embroidery stitches to create a textured design; Hardanger also is a region in Norway.

immigrant (IM-uh-gruhnt)—someone who comes from abroad to live permanently in a country

poultry (POHL-tree)—farm birds such as chickens and turkeys that farmers raise for their eggs and meat

rosemaling (ROZE-mohl-ing)—a Scandinavian design of painted flowers and scroll patterns

To Learn More

Collier, Christopher, and James Lincoln Collier. *A Century of Immigration: 1820–1924.* The Drama of American History. New York: Marshall Cavendish/Benchmark Books, 1999.

Hoobler, Dorothy, and Thomas Hoobler. *The Scandinavian American Family Album.* American Family Albums. New York: Oxford University Press, 1997.

McGill, Allyson. *The Swedish Americans.* The Immigrant Experience. Philadelphia: Chelsea House, 1997.

Paddock, Lisa Olson, and Carl Sokolnicki Rollyson. *A Student's Guide to Scandinavian American Genealogy.* American Family Tree. Phoenix, Ariz.: Oryx Press, 1996.

Places to Write and Visit

American Swedish Historical Museum
Franklin Delano Roosevelt Park
1900 Pattison Avenue
Philadelphia, PA 19145-5999

American Swedish Institute
2600 Park Avenue
Minneapolis, MN 55407-1007

The Danish Immigrant Museum
2212 Washington Street, P.O. Box 470
Elk Horn, IA 51531-0470

The National Genealogical Society
4527 17th Street North
Arlington, VA 22207-2399

The Norwegian-American Historical Association
1510 St. Olaf Avenue
Northfield, MN 55057-1097

Vesterheim Norwegian-American Museum
523 West Water Street
P.O. Box 379
Decorah, IA 52101-1733

Internet Sites

The American Swedish Institute
http://www.americanswedishinst.org

The Danish Immigrant Museum
http://dkmuseum.org

Family History
http://www.rootsweb.com/~cokids/index.htm

Gustavus Adolphus College
http://www.gac.edu/oncampus/academics/
scand-studies/scand-studies.cfm

Swedish American Museum Center
http://www.samac.org

Vesterheim Norwegian-American Museum
http://www.vesterheim.org

Index

Atlantic Ocean, 4, 5

Castle Garden, 15
choir, 26

Denmark, 4, 5, 7, 8, 9, 14, 16, 19, 29
disease, 11, 12, 17

Erie Canal, 16, 17

Great Lakes, 16, 17

Homestead Act, 17, 20
Hudson River, 16, 17
Humphrey, Hubert, 24, 29

Lindbergh, Charles, 23, 29

Mondale, Walter, 24, 29

New Sweden, 4
Nissen, Christopher, 22
Norway, 4, 5, 6, 7, 8, 9, 10, 16, 19

Peerson, Cleng, 4–6

Quakers, 4, 5

religion, 5, 11, 24

Sloopers, 5
smörgasbord, 26
soddys, 20
Sweden, 4, 5, 6, 7, 8, 9, 11, 12, 16, 18, 19, 24

DATE DUE

GAYLORD

PRINTED IN U.S.A.